H. Cauch

THE
Romance
of Roses

An Anthology of
Verse and Prose

LORENZ BOOKS
LONDON • NEW YORK • SYDNEY • BATH

First published in the UK in 1997 by Lorenz Books

© 1997 Anness Publishing Limited

Lorenz Books is an imprint of
Anness Publishing Limited
Hermes House
88-89 Blackfriars Road
London SE1 8HA

This edition published in Canada by Lorenz Books, distributed by
Raincoast Books Distribution Limited

ISBN 1 85967 333 3

A CIP catalogue record is available from the British Library

PUBLISHER: Joanna Lorenz
EDITORIAL MANAGER: Helen Sudell
DESIGNER: Nigel Partridge
TEXT COMPILED BY: Christine O'Brien
PICTURE RESEARCH BY: Vanessa Fletcher

Printed in China

1 3 5 7 9 10 8 6 4

CONTENTS

———

INTRODUCTION

"What's in a name?" asks Shakespeare's Juliet; "that which we call a rose by any other name would smell as sweet. So Romeo would, were he not Romeo call'd…" She is right, of course. The heady aroma of Damask and Musk roses scented the courts of the Indian emperors, just as the elusive odour of the Eglantine perfumes the summer hedgerows in temperate climates. But the name of the rose conjures up more than a fragrance.

To gardeners, the rose is the queen of flowers. Sturdy in her growth, exquisite in her shapes and colours, she finds a home in every bed, from the aristocratic parterre to the cottager's herb plot. Specialist breeders experiment with new varieties, and yet the old-fashioned forms have never lost their popularity.

For lovers, the rose expresses human feelings, its thorns translated into the pain of loss and its petals into the joys of courtship. For all of us, the rose is a reminder that even its long-lasting blossoms eventually fade and that we should appreciate such beauty while it is with us.

This celebration gathers together a few of the many words that have been written about the most highly prized of plants. Cultivated as carefully by the Ancient Greeks as by the early European settlers of the United States, roses have inspired poets, novelists and anonymous rhymers for thousands of years. The diversity of sources reflects that universal recognition which has made the rose an emblem of nations and a symbol of perfection, and has linked it eternally with ideal love and beauty.

∾ THE ∾
LOVERS' ROSE

The sweetest flower that blows,

I give you as we part.

For you it is a rose,

For me it is my heart.

FREDERICK PETERSON (1859–1938)

*F*or the Rose, ho, the Rose! is the eye of the flowers,
Is the blush of the meadows that feel themselves fair,
Is the lightning of beauty that strikes thro' the bowers,
On pale lovers who sit in the glow unaware.
Ho, the Rose breathes of love! ho, the Rose lifts the cup
To the red lips of Cypris invoked for a guest!
Ho! the Rose having curled its sweet leaves for the world,
Takes delight in the motion its petals keep up
As they laugh to the wind, as it laughs from the west!

TRANSLATED FROM SAPPHO (SIXTH CENTURY BC)

"BALLAD"

It was not in the winter
Our loving lot was cast!
It was the time of roses,
We plucked them as we passed!

That churlish season never frowned
On early lovers yet!
Oh no – the world was newly crowned
With flowers, when first we met.

'Twas twilight, and I bade you go,
But still you held me fast;
It was the time of roses,
We plucked them as we passed!

What else could peer my glowing cheek
That tears began to stud?
And when I asked the like of love
You snatched a damask bud,

And oped it to the dainty core
Still glowing to the last;
It was the time of roses,
We plucked them as we passed!

THOMAS HOOD (1799–1845)

*T*here fell a silvery-silken veil of light,
With quietude, and sultriness, and slumber,
Upon the upturn'd faces of a thousand
Roses that grew in an enchanted garden,
Where no wind dared to stir, unless on tiptoe –
Fell on the upturn'd faces of these roses
That gave out, in return for the love-light,
Their odorous souls in an ecstatic death –
Fell on the upturn'd faces of these roses
That smiled and died in this parterre, enchanted
By thee, and by the poetry of thy presence.

FROM *To Helen* BY EDGAR ALLAN POE (1809–49)

"LOVE AND FRIENDSHIP"

Love is like the wild rose-briar;
Friendship like the holly-tree.
The holly is dark when the rose-briar blooms,
But which will bloom most constantly?

The wild rose-briar is sweet in spring,
Its summer blossoms scent the air;
Yet wait till winter comes again,
And who will call the wild-briar fair?

Then, scorn the silly rose-wreath now,
And deck thee with the holly's sheen,
That, when December blights thy brow,
He may still leave thy garland green.

EMILY BRONTË (1818–48)

THE LOVERS' ROSE

I said to the rose, "The brief night goes
In babble and revel and wine.
O young lord-lover, what sighs are those,
For one that will never be thine?
But mine, but mine," so I sware to the rose,
"For ever and ever, mine."

And the soul of the rose went into my blood,
As the music clash'd in the hall;
And long by the garden lake I stood,
For I heard your rivulet fall
From the lake to the meadow and on to the wood,
Our wood, that is dearer than all...

FROM *MAUD* BY ALFRED, LORD TENNYSON (1809–92)

*T*he hard bitter feeling was getting pretty bad, when the maid brought in a box of flowers. Before she could speak, Annie had the cover off, and all were exclaiming at the lovely roses, heath, and ferns within.

"It's for Belle, of course; George always sends her some, but these are altogether ravishing," cried Annie, with a great sniff.

"They are for Miss March, the man said. And here's a note," put in the maid, holding it to Meg.

"What fun! Who are they from? Didn't know you had a lover," cried the girls, fluttering about Meg in a high state of curiosity and surprise.

"The note is from mother, and the flowers from Laurie," said Meg, simply, yet much gratified that he had not forgotten her.

"Oh indeed!" said Annie, with a funny look, as Meg slipped the note into her pocket, as a sort of talisman against envy, vanity, and false pride; for the few loving words had done her good, and the flowers cheered her up by their beauty.

FROM *LITTLE WOMEN* BY LOUISA MAY ALCOTT (1832–88)

"JUNE"

June. Mine is the Month of Roses; yes and mine
The Month of Marriages! All pleasant sights
And scents, the fragrance of the blossoming vine,
The foliage of the valleys and the heights.
Mine are the longest days, the loveliest nights;
The mower's scythe makes music to my ear;
I am the mother of all dear delights;
I am the fairest daughter of the year.

HENRY WADSWORTH
LONGFELLOW (1807–82)

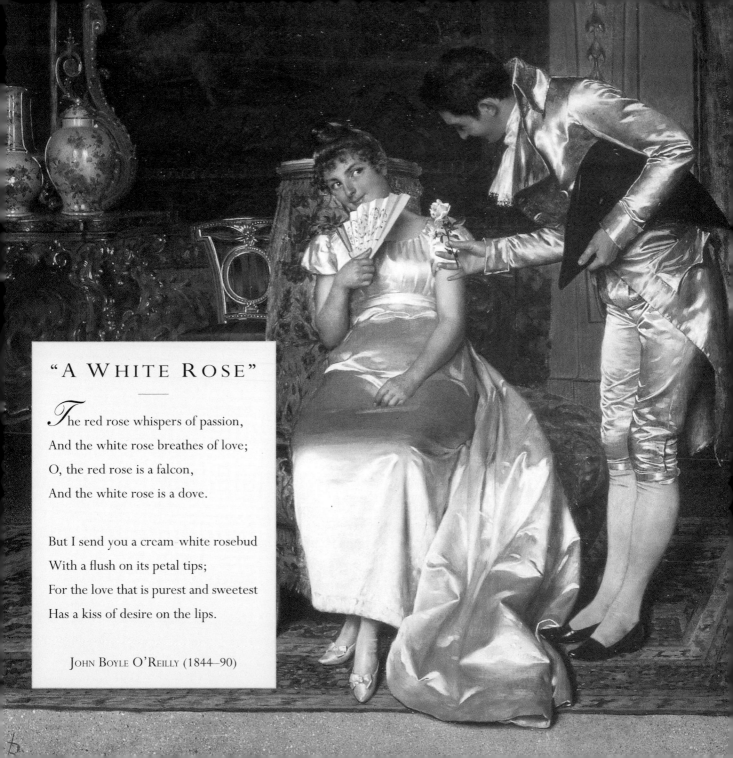

"A White Rose"

The red rose whispers of passion,
And the white rose breathes of love;
O, the red rose is a falcon,
And the white rose is a dove.

But I send you a cream white rosebud
With a flush on its petal tips;
For the love that is purest and sweetest
Has a kiss of desire on the lips.

JOHN BOYLE O'REILLY (1844–90)

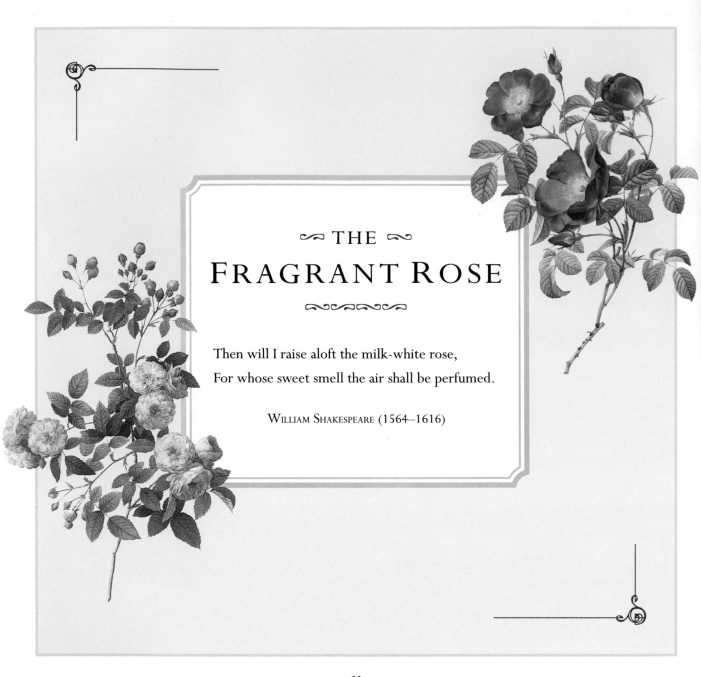

ᕌ THE ᕍ
FRAGRANT ROSE

Then will I raise aloft the milk-white rose,
For whose sweet smell the air shall be perfumed.

WILLIAM SHAKESPEARE (1564–1616)

"Here is a new kind of rose, which I found this morning in the garden," said she, choosing a small crimson one from among the flowers in the vase. "There will be but five or six on the bush this season. This is the most perfect of them all; not a speck of blight or mildew on it. And how sweet it is! – sweet like no other rose! One can never forget that scent!"

"Ah! – let me see! – let me hold it!" cried the guest, eagerly seizing the flower, which, by the spell peculiar to remembered odors, brought innumerable associations along with the fragrance that it exhaled. "Thank you! This has done me good. I remember how I used to prize this flower, – long ago, I suppose, very long ago! – or was it only yesterday? It makes me feel young again…"

FROM *THE HOUSE OF THE SEVEN GABLES* BY

NATHANIEL HAWTHORNE (1804–64)

I smelt and prays'd the fragrant rose,

Blushing, thus answer'd she:

The praise you gave,

The scent I have,

Does not belong to mee;

This harmless odour, none

But only God indeed does owne;

To be his keepers, my poor leaves he chose;

And thus reply'd the rose.

FROM *TRIVIAL POEMS AND TRIOLETS* (1651)

BY PATRICK CAREY

$\mathscr{A}$ romantic Mogul legend from India describes how the essential oil of roses was discovered. Recently married, the Emperor Jehangir and his bride were walking in the beautiful gardens surrounding their palace, where the long pools of water had been filled with roses to celebrate their wedding. As they stood to savour the perfumed air, they noticed that the heat of the sun on the petals had produced a film of oil that floated on the surface. So wonderful was the scent of the oil that they ordered it to be bottled and this attar was ever after the scent of the emperors.

∽ 27 ∽

O, how much more doth beauty beauteous seem
By that sweet ornament which truth doth give!
The rose looks fair, but fairer we it deem
For that sweet odour which doth in it live.
The canker-blooms have full as deep a dye
As the perfumed tincture of the roses,
Hang on such thorns, and play as wantonly
When Summer's breath their masked buds discloses:
But, for their virtue only is their show,
They live unwoo'd, and unrespected fade;
Die to themselves. Sweet roses do not so;
Of their sweet deaths are sweetest odours made:
And so of you, beauteous and lovely youth,
When that shall fade, my verse distils your truth.

Sonnet 54 by William Shakespeare (1564–1616)

To Make Little Cusshins of Parfumed Roses

Take buddes of redde Roses, their heades and
toppes cut awaye, drie them in the shadowe upon
a table, or a linnen cloath: water and sprinkle the
sayde buddes with Rose water, and let them drie,
doynge this five or sixe times, turning them alwayes, to the
end they waxe not mouldy: than take the poudre of Cipre, Muske
& Amber, made into a pouder according as you woulde make
them excellent, for the more you put in of it the better they
shal be: put to it also lignum aloes well beaten in pouder. Let
the saide pouder be put with the budds wete with rose water,
mixing well the budds together with the pouder, to thend al
may be wel incorporated, so shall you leave them so al a night,
covering them with som linnen cloth, or Taffeta that the musk may not breath or rise
out. The whiche thing done, take finallye lyttle bagges of Taffeta of what bignesse you
wil, and according to the quantitie of the buddes that you would put among all the
pouder. Then close up the bagges…

FROM *Delights for Ladies* BY SIR HUGH PLATT (1552–1608)

❧ THE ❧
QUEEN OF
FLOWERS

The cowslip is a country wench,

The violet is a nun;

But I will woo the dainty rose,

The queen of everyone.

THOMAS HOOD (1799–1845)

Within the garden's peaceful scene
Appear'd two lovely foes,
Aspiring to the rank of queen –
The Lily and the Rose.

The Rose soon redden'd into rage,
And, swelling with disdain,
Appeal'd to many a poet's page
To prove her right to reign.

The Lily's height bespoke command –
A fair imperial flow'r;
She seem'd design'd for Flora's hand,
The sceptre of her pow'r.

This civil bick'ring and debate
The goddess chanc'd to hear.
And flew to save, ere yet too late,
The pride of the pareterre.

Your's is, she said, the nobler hue,
And your's the statelier mien,
And, till a third surpasses you,
Let each be deem'd the queen.

FROM *THE LILY AND THE ROSE* BY WILLIAM COWPER (1731–1800)

The only hereditary monarchs who have withstood the test of time in public opinion were established by poets: the lion is always the king of beasts, the eagle the monarch of the skies, and the rose the queen of flowers. The first two of these, being based upon and upheld by force, have, in their very nature, reason enough to explain the length of time they have lasted; the sovereignty of the rose, less fiercely imposed and more freely accepted, implies a greater flattery with regard to the throne and a greater honour with regard to those who established her there.

FROM *LES ROSES* (1824) ILLUSTRATED BY P. J. REDOUTÉ,

TEXT BY C. A. THORRY

You violets that first appeare,
By your pure purple mantles known,
Like the proud virgins of the yeare
As if the spring were all your owne,
What are you when the Rose is blown?

SIR HENRY WOTTON (1568–1639)

IN THIS SOLEMN RANDEVOUX OF FLOWERS AND HERBS, THE ROSE STOOD FORTH, AND MADE AN ORATION TO THIS EFFECT

*I*t is not unknown to you, how I have precedency of all flowers, confirmed unto me under the patent of a double sence, sight and smell. What more curious colours? how do all diers blush, when they behold my blushing as conscious to themselves that their art cannot imitate that tincture, which nature hath stamped upon me. Smell, it is not lusciously offensive, nor dangerously faint, but comforteth with a delight, and delighteth with the comfort thereof: yea, when dead, I am more soveraigne than living: what cordials are made of my syrups? how many corrupted lungs (those fans of nature) sore wasted with consumtion that they seem utterly unable any longer to

cool the heat of the heart, with their ventilation, are with conserves made of my stamped leaves, restored to their former soundess again. More would I say in my own cause, but that happily I may be taxed of pride, and self-flattery, who speake much in mine own behalf, and therefore I leave the rest to the judgement of such as hear me…

FROM *ANTHEOLOGIA, OR THE SPEECH OF FLOWERS* BY THOMAS FULLER (1608–61)

THE QUEEN OF FLOWERS

✿ ✿ ✿ ✿ ✿ ✿

*T*here were great quantities of roses, lovelier than any under the heavens; there were little closed buds and some slightly larger; and there were some of another size coming into their season and nearly ready to open: these are not to be rejected. The large open roses are all gone in a day but the buds remain quite fresh for at least two or three days. These buds were very beautiful to me: nowhere had such lovely flowers ever grown. Whoever succeeded in laying hold of one should value it very highly; if I could have a garland of them no treasure would please me more.

FROM *THE ROMANCE OF THE ROSE* BY GUILLAUME DE LORRIS (MID-THIRTEENTH CENTURY)

Garlands for Queens, maybe –
Laurels – for rare degree
Of soul or sword.
Ah – but remembering me –
Ah – but remembering thee –
Nature in chivalry –
Nature in charity –
Nature in equity –
The Rose ordained!

EMILY DICKINSON (1830–86)

*L*ike Breath from heaven's own portals

Come Roses bright to mortals;

The Graces sound their praises:

The Loves in flow'ry mazes

Each one, his voice upraises,

To Sing with joy Cithera's toy.

Plant pleasing to the Muses,

With love all song infuses;

The fragrance from its treasure

It pours with equal measure

On him, whose touch is pleasure,

Or him who strays in thorny ways.

ODE 51, DEDICATED TO THE ROSE BY ANACREON

(C. 580–490 BC)

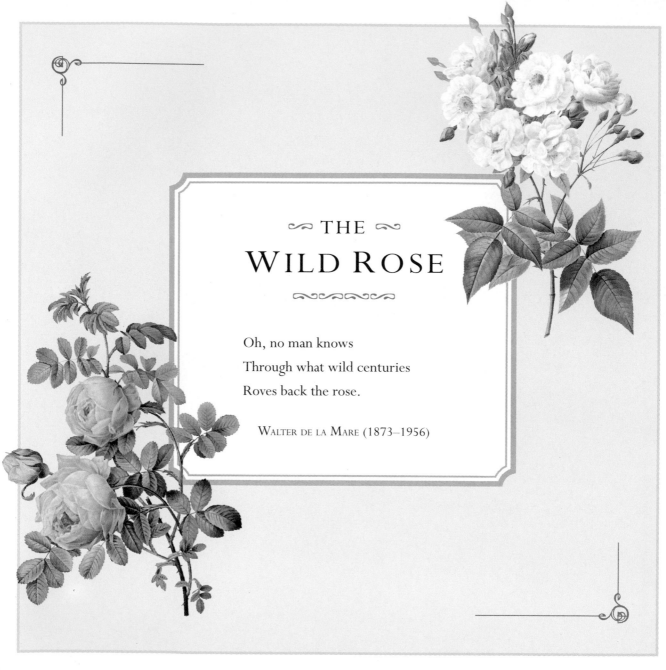

THE
WILD ROSE

Oh, no man knows
Through what wild centuries
Roves back the rose.

WALTER DE LA MARE (1873–1956)

The Eglantine, a variety of wild rose, was widely planted in the early settlements in the United States because it grew quickly, could be clipped into a fragrant hedge and had a long life. In 1689, William Penn wrote to John Blackwell at Pennsbury: "Plow no more land than serves the house. Let the Gardiner, when come, take special care of getting quick setts and good speedy and quick shades… Let him plant wt. grows quickest, be sure woodbine and sweet brier, etc."

Legend has it that Penn took eighteen roses with him when he travelled from England to America for the second time.

A rose-bud by my early walk
Adown a corn-enclosed bawk
Sae gently bent its thorny stalk,
All on a dewy morning.

Ere twice the shades o' dawn are fled,
In a' its crimson glory spread
And drooping rich the dewy head,
It scents the early morning.

FROM *A ROSE-BUD BY MY EARLY WALK* BY
ROBERT BURNS (1759–96)

*W*e may add that the fortunate possessor of a Herb-garden finds it an ideal refuge for any of the odds and ends of plants that interest him… Here, too, we may enjoy such old-fashioned Roses as were valued for their sweetness, and are banished in these days, when, owing a good deal to the demands of Flower-shows, size, form, and colour are put before fragrance. Who is going to make a pound of pot-pourri (worth having) out of a whole tentful of fashionable Roses? In the herb-garden we would have the Moss-Rose, the Damask-Rose, and the Cabbage-

Rose. The Cabbage-Rose makes the best rose-water, and the Wild-briar, or Dog-Rose, is one of the most valuable for its curative qualities… And why should we not have Sweetbriar? If we do, we must remember it hates formality and confinement. Give it the wildest and most open place.

FROM *THE HERB-GARDEN* (1911) BY
FRANCES BARDSWELL

I saw the sweetest flower wild nature yields,
A fresh blown musk-Rose. 'Twas the first that threw
Its sweets upon the summer; graceful it grew
As is the wand that queen Titania wields.
And, as I feasted on its fragrancy,
I thought the garden-rose it far excelled.

FROM *TO A FRIEND WHO SENT ME SOME ROSES* BY
JOHN KEATS (1795–1821)

*N*obody knows this little Rose

It might a pilgrim be

Did I not take it from the ways

And lift it up to thee.

Only a Bee will miss it —

Only a Butterfly,

Hastening from far journey —

On its breast to lie —

Only a Bird will wonder —

Only a Breeze will sigh —

Ah Little Rose — how easy

For such as thee to die.

EMILY DICKINSON (1830–86)

Queen of her sisters is the Wild Rose,

Sprung from the earnest sun and ripe young June;

The year's own darling and the Summer's Queen!

Lustrous as the new throned crescent moon.

Much of that early prophet look she shows,

Mixed with her fair espoused blush which glows,

As if the ethereal fairy blood were seen;

Like a soft evening over sunset snows,

Half twilight violet shade, half crimson sheen.

FROM *THE WILD ROSE AND THE SNOWDROP* BY

GEORGE MEREDITH (1828–1909)

~ THE ~
ROSE THAT
FADES AND DIES

A rose, bent by the wind and pricked by thorns, yet has its heart turned upwards.

HUNA (c. 216–297 AD)

"AN OCTOBER GARDEN"

In my Autumn garden I was fain

To mourn among my scattered roses;

Alas for that lost rosebud that uncloses

To Autumn's languid sun and rain

When all the world is on the wane!

Which has not felt the sweet constraint of June,

Nor heard the nightingale in tune.

Broad-faced asters by my garden walk,

You are but coarse compared with roses:

More choice, more dear that rosebud which uncloses,

Faint-scented, pinched, upon its stalk,

That least and last which cold winds balk;

A rose it is though least and last of all,

A rose to me though at the fall.

CHRISTINA ROSSETTI (1830–94)

The rose, at edge of winter now,
Doth fade with all its summer glow;
Old are become the roses all,
Decline to age we also shall;

And with this prayer I'll end my lay,
Amen, with me, O Parry say;
To us be rest from all annoy,
And a robust old age of joy.

FROM *THE INVITATION* BY GORONWY OWEN (1723–69)

*D*uring the eighteenth century, many fine gardens were established in America. Among them was the garden at The Woodlands, near Philadelphia, owned by William Hamilton, a rose-lover. While he was on a visit to London in 1785, it appears that Hamilton received a letter from his private secretary at The Woodlands, telling him that several of his plants had died. In reply, he wrote as follows: "Am I to infer that all the plants included under those numbers are dead – pray are none of the eastern plane, the Portugal laurels (between 500 and 600), the evergreen sweet Briar, Singletons Rose, the evergreen Rose, the moscheute double rose, the white Damask rose, the variegated damask rose, the yellow Austrian Rose, the Burgundy rose, the monthly Portland rose, the monthly red rose and the monthly variegated rose – now living?"

"THE FUNERALL RITES OF THE ROSE"

The Rose was sick and smiling di'd;

And (being to be sanctifi'd)

About the Bed, there sighing stood

The sweet, the flowrie Sisterhood.

Some hung their heads, while some did bring

(To wash her) water from the Spring.

Some laid her forth, while others wept,

But all a solemne Fast there kept.

The holy Sisters, some among

The sacred *Dirge* and *Trentall* sung.

But ah! what sweets smelt everywhere,

As Heaven had spent all perfumes there

At last, when prayers for the dead,

And Rites were all accomplished;

They, weeping, spread a lawnie loome,

And clos'd her up, as in a Toombe.

ROBERT HERRICK (1591–1674)

"SONG"

Weep, as if you thought of laughter!
Smile, as tears were coming after!
Marry your pleasures to your woes;
And think life's green well worth its rose!

No sorrow will your heart betide,
Without a comfort by its side;
The sun may sleep in his sea-bed,
But you have starlight overhead.

Trust not to Joy! the rose of June,
When opened wide, will wither soon;
Italian days without twilight
Will turn them suddenly to night.

Joy, most changeful of all things,
Flits away on rainbow wings;
And when they look the gayest know
It is that they are spread to go!

ELIZABETH BARRETT BROWNING (1806–61)

ACKNOWLEDGEMENTS

The Publishers thank the agencies below for permission to reproduce the following images:

Fine Art Photographic Library, London:
p. 5 Emile Vernon, *Marguerite*; p.9 George Lawrence Bulleid, *A Bouquet of Roses*; p. 10 Henry Thomas Schäfer, *The Time of Roses*, Private Collection; p.13 Mabel Ashby, *A Blooming Relationship, A Rosy Future*; p. 15 Adrian Stokes, *Contemplation*, Private Collection; p.16 Abbey Altson, *An Arabian Fantasy*, Baumkotter Gallery; p.18 Federigo Andreotti, *An Interesting Letter*, Burlington Paintings; p.20 Anonymous, *The Wedding*; p.21 Vittorio Reggianini, *La Rose*, Galerie Berko; p.23 Victor Gabriel Gilbert, *In the Rose Garden*, Galerie Berko; p.24 Luigi Maggiorani, *Elegant Ladies Gathering Roses*, Galerie Berko; p.26 Harry Watson, *Roses*, City Wall Gallery; p.27 Rudolph Ernst, *The Perfume Makers*; p. 30 Albert Sorkau, *The Perfume Makers*; p.33 Emile Vernon,

English Rose; p. 37 Henry Thomas Schäfer, *The Time of Roses*, Gavin Graham Gallery; p. 40 Sir Lawrence Alma-Tadema, *Rose of all the Roses*; p. 43 Ernest Normand, *Evil Sought*, Private Collection; p.45 Emile Vernon, *Picking Roses*; p. 46 Herman Seeger, *Summer's Delight*, Anthony Mitchell Paintings; p. 47 William Kay Blacklock, *Gathering Wild Flowers*; p.48 (right) Henry John Yeend King,

Cottage Gardeners; p.51 Ernest Rudolf Meyer, *A Study of Pink Roses and Butterflies*; p. 52 Thomas Ralph Spence, *The Sleeping Beauty*, Paisnel Gallery; p. 55 Emile Vernon, *A Summer Reverie*, Anthony Mitchell Paintings; p. 57 Robert Gordon, *Pruning Roses*.

Visual Arts Library, London: p. 2 Eugène Henri Cauchois, *Roses*; p. 6 Johan Laurentz Jensen, *Roses in a Basket on the Table*; p. 14 Eduard Niczky, *The Lady and the Rose*; p. 19 Auguste Renoir, *Still Life with Bouquet*, Houston Museum of Fine Art; p. 28 Viggo Langer, *The Rose Garden*; p. 34 Johan Laurentz Jensen, *Roses*; p. 38 Johan Laurentz Jensen, *Roses in a Basket under a Rose Bush*; p. 41 George Dunlop Leslie, *The Rose Queen*; p. 42 Dante Gabriel Rossetti, *The Roman Window*, Museo de Arte de Ponce; p. 58 Johan Laurentz Jensen, *Bouquet of Roses*; p. 59 Johan Laurentz Jensen, *Roses*; p. 61 L. Bouvier Bardelli, *Yellow and Pink Roses*; p. 62 Auguste Renoir, *Roses by the Window*.